Golden Nuggets

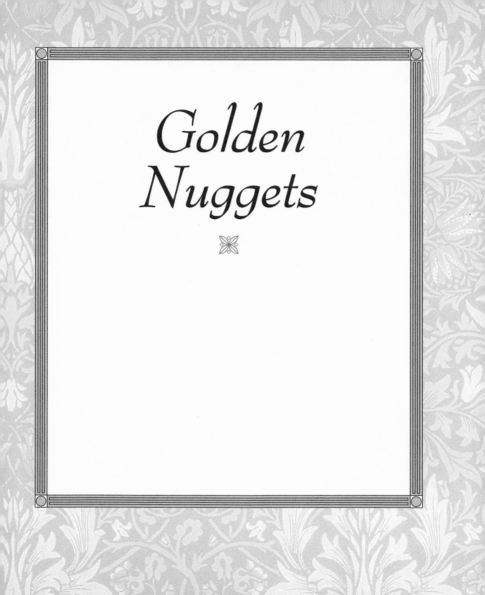

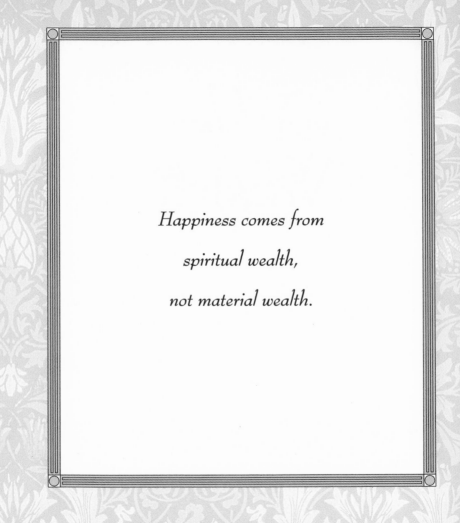

Happiness comes from

spiritual wealth,

not material wealth.

Golden Nuggets

from Sir John Templeton

Templeton Foundation Press
Philadelphia and London

TEMPLETON FOUNDATION PRESS
Two Radnor Corporate Center, Suite 320
100 Matsonford Road
Radnor, Pennsylvania 19087

Printed in the United States of America
Library of Congress Catalog Card Number: 97-90754
ISBN 1-890151-04-1

Designed by
Joanna Hill and Helene Krasney

"Snakeshead" pattern, used on dust jacket
and in book, are by William Morris,
used with permission of V & A Picture Library.

Contents

Introduction

People are asking many important questions today:

How do I find peace in the midst of turmoil?
How can I be in the world, but not of the world?
How can my life be useful and happy?
What is true prosperity?

Finding the answers to these questions is an important part of life. "Seek and you shall find" are words of wisdom that lead you on a search for true values and what I call "laws of life." The material presented here represents some principles I have used for making personal, professional, and spiritual decisions. It is designed to inspire as well as encourage you; to help you consider more deeply the laws you personally live by; and to reap the rewards of their practical application.

The world operates on spiritual principles just as it operates on the laws of physics and gravity. It is up to us to learn what these principles are and then choose to live by them. Spiritual laws are impartial because they apply equally to everyone throughout the world. They work without prejudice or bias at all times and in all places. These laws are self-enforcing and are not dependent on human authority or commandments.

Golden Nuggets is aimed at assisting people of all ages to learn more about these universal truths of life that transcend modern times or particular cultures in the hope that it may help people to make their lives happier and more useful. There is a relationship between the invisible thoughts and feelings of our minds and the visible actions we take as a result of them. If we learn how things work, we will be better able to live productive, joyful lives.

You will see there are several themes that run through this collection: themes of thankfulness, gratitude, prayer, forgiveness, and positive thinking. These represent simple wisdom that has taken a lifetime to gather. It would be a great joy to me if I could share with you a few words that might make your lives more peaceful and loving.

It has been said that "life is a tough school because the exams come first and the learning afterwards." This book is a sincere attempt to provide some opportunities for learning so you will be prepared for the exams that will come.

If this book has been useful for you, there is a larger, more extensive version available called *Worldwide Laws of Life: 200 Eternal Spiritual Principles*.

It is a collection of two hundred laws of life that I have gathered from ancient scripture, philosophers, storytellers, scientists, artists, and historians. You can probably find it at your favorite bookstore.

Our stay on this small planet called Earth is a brief one, and we have an excellent opportunity to leave the world a better place than we found it through our choice of how we live our lives. When we examine our thoughts, words, and deeds, and align them with principles that work, not only for ourselves but also for others, we know we are on the right track. I sincerely hope that these words help you to live a life that is loving, peaceful, prosperous, and useful.

JOHN MARKS TEMPLETON

Thanksgiving

Thanksgiving is a creative force that, if
lived on a continuous basis and not just for one
day each year, can create more good in your life.
Perhaps we could call this way of life thanksliving.

Thanksliving is based on the premise that living
a life of appreciation and gratefulness leads to
having more to be thankful for. We have the ability
to create blessings in our lives
through the power of our minds
and the choices we make.

Thanksgiving opens the door
to spiritual growth.

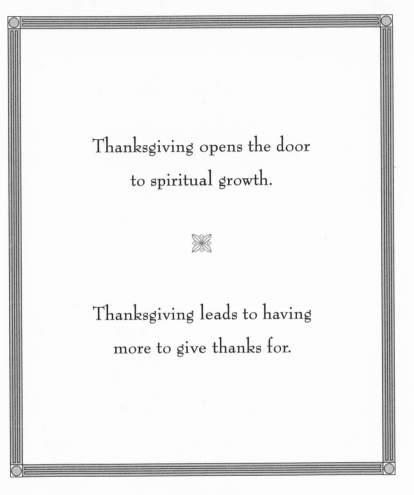

Thanksgiving leads to having
more to give thanks for.

Praise, not complaining, increases the good

and the blessing in whatever it is directed toward.

When we speak words of praise as our consistent, joyous

response to life, we increase the good and

draw out the best in others.

This law of life is about combining

the expectations of the mind with the power

of the heart. Let us use the laws of thanksgiving

to bless ourselves and others and make

our lives more complete.

Thanksgiving, not complaining,
attracts people to you.

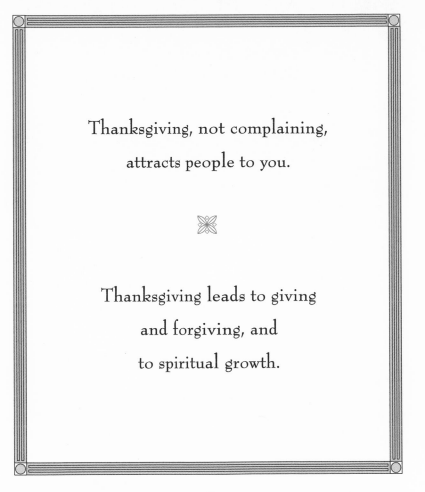

Thanksgiving leads to giving
and forgiving, and
to spiritual growth.

Do you awaken every morning
with a song of praise on your lips? Do you feel
full of appreciation for life as you live it every day?
Or do you have to think long and hard before
finding something to be grateful for?

When we are grateful for the blessings
we already have, our very gratitude attracts extra
good to us. Gratitude nurtures within us a positive,
joy-filled consciousness and unifies us
with life's flow, which gives birth
to inner fulfillment.

An attitude of gratitude
creates blessings.

Count your blessings and you will have
an attitude of gratitude.

Forgiveness
& Prayer

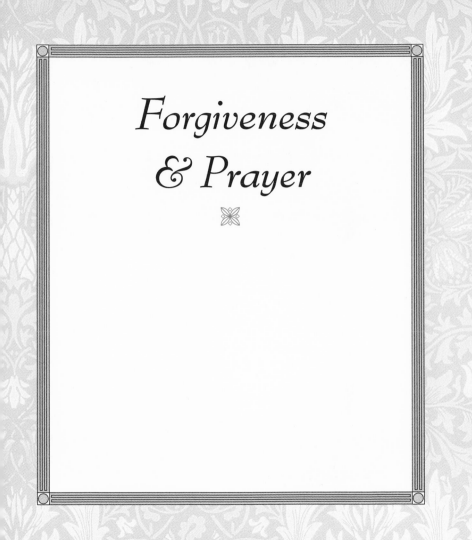

Forgiveness plays a vital role
in our life. It may take varying lengths
of time for us to realize that the spiral of holding
more tightly to hurts we have sustained only brings
grief to all parties, ourselves included.

Forgiveness can be about knowing that although we
experience pain, we don't have to experience long-term
suffering. The faith expressed through giving thanks
for our challenges can help dissolve the appearance
of negative circumstances and, as we
give thanks and forgive, we are uplifted.

Forgiveness benefits both the
giver and the receiver.

To be forgiven,
you must first forgive.

Forgiving uplifts the forgiver.

An important thing to remember is that

whatever kind of confusion may be around you,

what is within your own consciousness is what counts.

And you have available two of the most powerful tools

to use—love and prayer.

Prayer has been described as a concerted effort

for the physical consciousness to become attuned to the

consciousness of the Creator. By communicating with

God on a regular basis, we may receive guidance

and the power to understand as well as receive

an increase of energy to do the will of God.

12

You have the most powerful

weapons on earth—

love and prayer.

Through prayer you receive

spiritual energy.

Positive Thinking

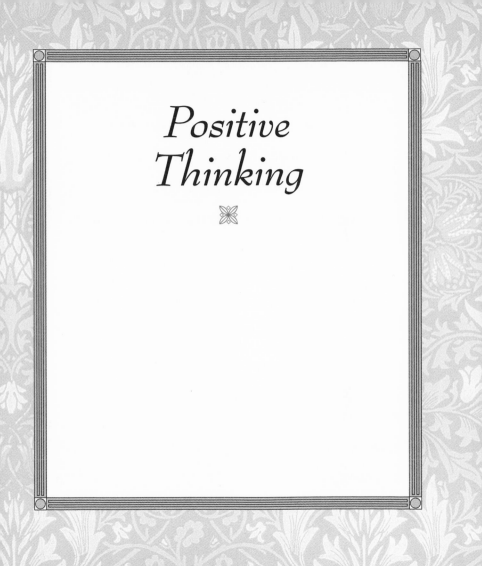

If we see the good in everyone and everything,

and appreciate the beauty that is all around us,

a kind of magical transformation begins to work

in our lives. It is a law of life that whatever we give

our attention to, and believe, becomes our experience.

Concentrate your thoughts on the good,

the beautiful, and the true things of life. This

positive attitude can help you perceive the presence

of God active in your life and put into operation

the divine magic that can open doors

to greater usefulness and joy.

Beautiful thoughts
build a beautiful soul.

A measure of mental health
is the disposition
to find good everywhere.

It has been said that "to enthuse" means to "fill with spirit." The energy of enthusiasm is similar to a radio signal that carries around the world. It can be transmitted and received.

The individual who takes up any activity as a positive adventure can inspire the same attitude in others. Although no one can be sunny all the time, if we take up our tasks with enthusiasm, it is likely those around us may also catch our spirit.

18

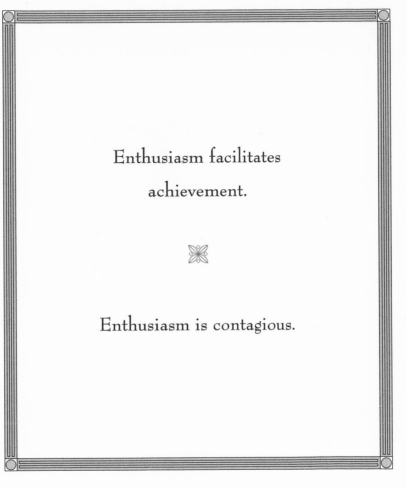

Enthusiasm facilitates
achievement.

Enthusiasm is contagious.

A problem that occurs in your life may simply be a question that life asks you. However, anxiety can make solutions seem elusive, and pessimism can be a block to embracing the part of ourselves that already knows the answers. Your positive outlook can open doors to opportunity that fear might otherwise tightly lock.

By choosing to look for the good in all situations, we can place our attention on workable solutions to problems rather than focusing on what we perceive as wrong.

Expect the best and your positive
outlook opens the door to opportunity.

You find what you look for:
good or evil,
problems or solutions.

Love

M*any people needlessly seem to make their lives difficult by failing to realize the importance of the thoughts and attitudes they send out. Begin cleaning out those things in your mind that you know make for more problems, such as resentment, self-pity, blaming others, anger.*

Know that there is no power in the universe greater than love, and no act more important than loving. Agape *is the unselfish love that gives of itself and expects nothing in return. It is the love that grows as you give it to others.*

24

You get back what you give out.

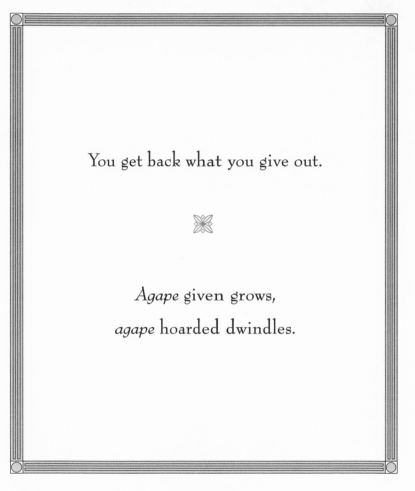

Agape given grows,
agape hoarded dwindles.

One of the keys of prosperity is realizing that

true prosperity doesn't come by getting more—

it comes by giving more! The universe holds nothing

back from the one who lovingly and sincerely gives.

To allow a full and free flow of love from the heart

into life can be a secret of rich and satisfying living.

In fact, giving more love can be a turning point for the

soul, one of those blessed moments when the hardships

of life's adversity give way to awakening to the presence

of God. Letting go of those blockages can open

wide the doorway for even greater giving of our love.

26

By giving you grow.

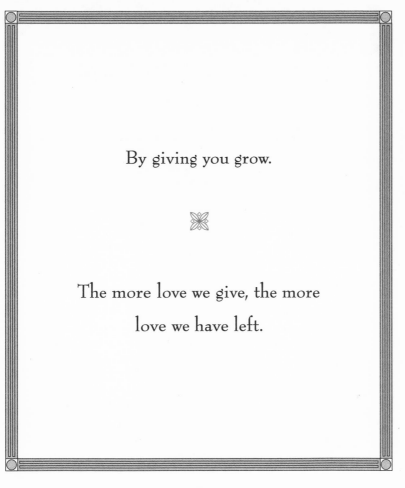

The more love we give, the more
love we have left.

G*iving love consciously through thoughts,
words, and deeds can help you to become your own
force-field of love. The gift, the giving, and the receiving
can be one harmonious flow of the most
powerful force in the universe.*

*Often, being a blessing requires nothing more than a
word of encouragement and hope to someone who may be
experiencing discouragement and despair. A real part of our
life's work may be to help others' burdens become easier
to bear, and what a wonderful awareness to know that as
we open ourselves to rich blessings, those blessings flow
through the channel of our love to bless and help others.*

Love given is love received.

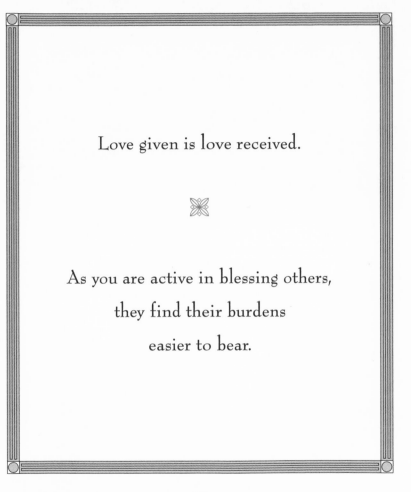

As you are active in blessing others,
they find their burdens
easier to bear.

Loneliness cannot be overcome by getting something; it must be remedied by giving something! Opportunities are limitless when one seeks to fill a need in humanity. Beginning with one effort, such as spending an unselfish hour with someone less fortunate, can produce a miracle for the giver and the receiver.

When you love your work and hold the attitude that what you do may be done on behalf of others, your life and your work can take on special meaning and deep significance. People who use their talents to help and love others less fortunate will be rewarded and find success.

30

You cannot be lonely
if you help the lonely.

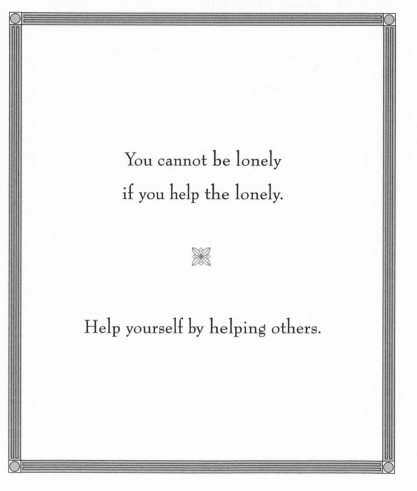

Help yourself by helping others.

To be liked and appreciated is a natural and deep-seated human desire. So, the experience of getting along well with others is no small matter. It is an important skill that must be mastered if we are to be effective and happy. The answer may appear simple, but it is extremely vital: to sincerely like people.

The gifts of love, joy, peace, patience, kindness, goodness, faithfulness, gentleness, and self-control are gifts of a humble and sincere individual and come directly from the heart.

You are sought after
if you reflect love, joy, peace,
patience, kindness, goodness,
faithfulness, gentleness
and self-control.

Humility

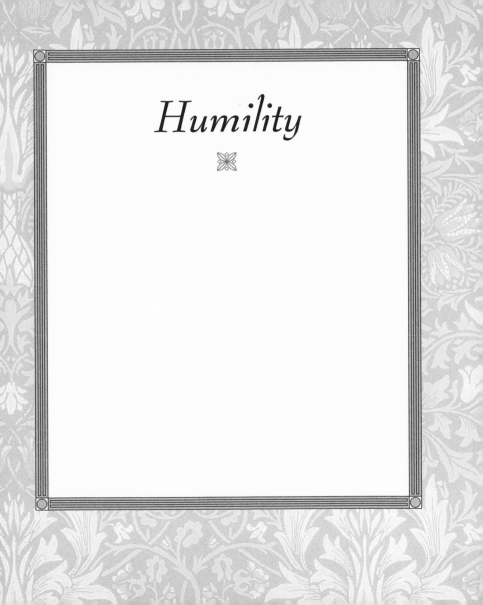

A successful life involves personal relationships,

family experiences, and spiritual involvement, as well

as our professional lives. There may be many life possibilities

for each of us. Success is finding out which of these may be

the most meaningful, working hard for these dreams, and

giving credit for the help and guidance necessary to fulfill them.

Those great people who are among the most respected

acknowledge that their greatness comes not from their

personal self, but from a higher power working through them.

The true meaning of humility is knowing that the

personal self is a vehicle of a higher power.

36

Give credit and help to all
who have helped you.

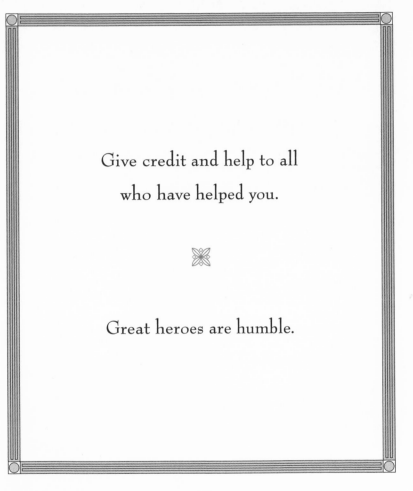

Great heroes are humble.

Humility is the key to true progress. When we can begin to sense the wonder of creation, in the beauty of the stars and the glory of the trees and flowers, we experience a state of awe and wonder. We can glimpse that God infinitely exceeds our comprehension and understanding. As we realize how little we know and how much there is to learn, this is the beginning of humility.

True humility can lead us into a prayerful attitude, and prayer can bring us in tune with the Infinite. A person who is genuinely humble and grateful for God-given blessings opens the door to a kind of heaven on earth, here and now.

Humility leads to prayer as well as
progress and brings you in tune
with the Infinite.

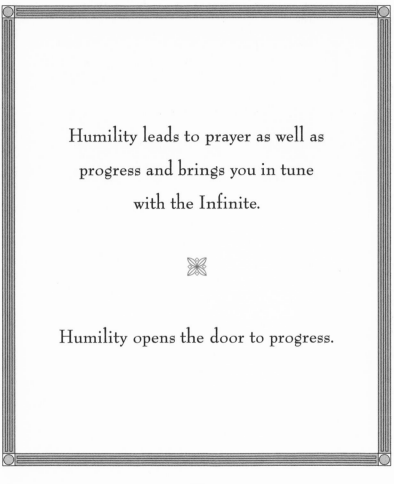

Humility opens the door to progress.

The idea of humility and the humble approach to life admits that the universe and all creatures within it may be manifestations of infinite creative power. When we are permeated with a lively faith and a sincere desire to learn, messages of love and guidance flow to us and through us like a beautiful river that has found smooth passage through our life stream.

To find contentment in the heart and a sense of fulfillment in the mind, it becomes important that we learn to praise and affirm life and the goodness of living.

If you think you know it all,
you are less likely to learn more.

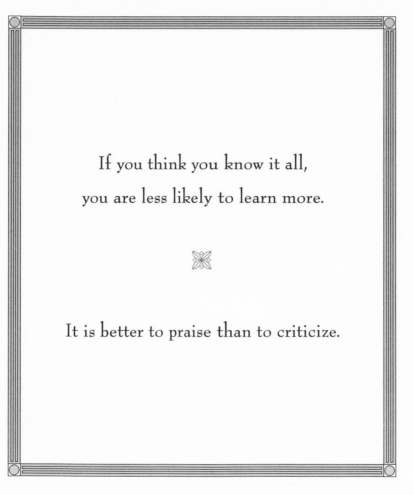

It is better to praise than to criticize.

Science is revealing to us an exciting world in dynamic flux, whose mechanisms are ever more baffling and staggering in their beauty and complexity. The quantity of knowledge that has become known within the last century is said to be greater than all of that discovered since the beginning of humanity.

And yet there is so much we do not know! What would happen if research foundations and religious institutions would begin to devote energy to scientific studies into the spiritual realm? Could we create even more potential for humans to make progress if we were able to increase our knowledge of spiritual information?

42

Our quantity of spiritual knowledge
is smaller than Ptolemy's knowledge
of astronomy.

✳

The unknown is not unknowable and
is vastly greater than the known.

Happiness

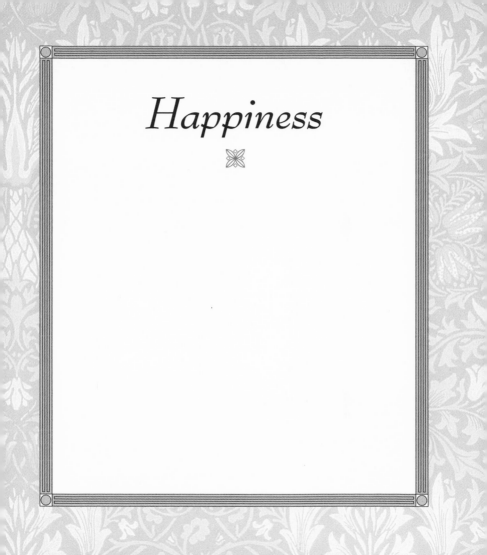

B*egin to practice the belief that you have a significant part to play in life and take steps to discover what that is. When an opportunity comes to express your talent, welcome that opportunity to live a life that gives inspiration and service to others. "Seek and you shall find" is excellent guidance for living a productive life!*

Each of us is born with the freedom to choose the thoughts that direct our lives. We may choose either the path of negative attitudes or loving, positive ones. When we choose to fill our minds and hearts with the goodness of life, and turn our backs to lesser things, we choose to live in heaven on earth!

46

The secret of a productive life
can be sought and found.

You can build your own heaven
or hell on earth.

People devote much time and energy to seeking happiness, but the sad fact is that we are often seeking it outside ourselves. Actually, the happiest people are those who are working to give happiness to others. Happiness is not found by seeking it; it is a by-product of caring about other people.

True and lasting happiness comes from spiritual wealth because, with it, we have a resource to draw upon. With spiritual wealth as the foundation and security for our lives, we gain a deep and abiding peace that cannot be obtained with material wealth alone.

48

Happiness is always a by-product.

Happiness comes from
spiritual wealth,
not material wealth.

If we live to share our special talents and serve others instead of just accumulating material wealth, we can find happiness from the joy of freely giving. Although happiness as a goal unto itself is an empty one, it can be our companion on the road to fulfilling our destiny in this world.

However, we will probably not live the useful, joyful lives that are possible if we do not know where we are going. With clear direction, and with loving attitudes toward ourselves and others, we can achieve much in our lives by having a focus for our life's work.

50

Happiness pursued, eludes;
happiness given, returns.

If you do not know what you
want to achieve with your life,
you may not achieve much.

Real joy is a deep and lasting quality that helps transcend difficulties and restores a zest for life and living no matter what happens. People who are trapped in envy are often those who look for joy outside themselves and resent others for the talents and possessions they might have.

When we begin to realize that joy comes from within us, we can communicate this joy to others and also gain a wonderful feeling of confidence in knowing that others may receive happiness from the expressions we give to life!

Joy provides assurance;
envy brings loneliness.

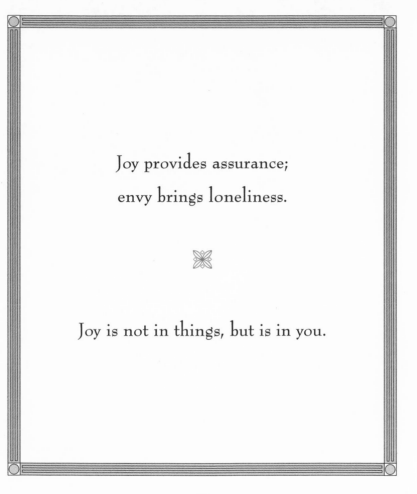

Joy is not in things, but is in you.

Progress

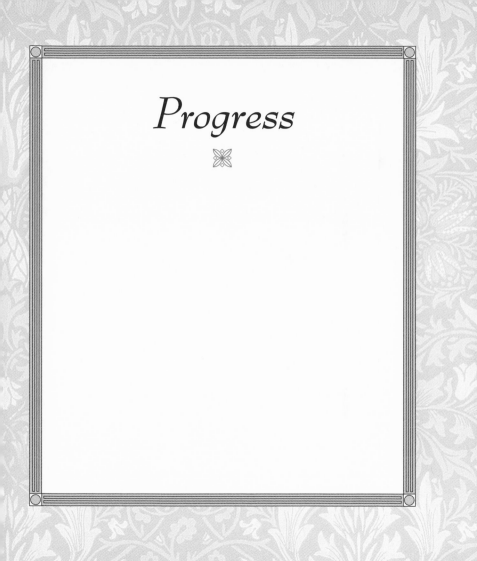

Wherever we are and whatever we are doing, it is possible to learn something that can enrich our lives and the lives of others. It may be necessary to release outmoded ways of thinking and acting in order to try something new but, when we do, life becomes more exciting and fulfilling than we dreamed possible.

We can all learn from the experiences in life, and we can also learn from not learning when life gives us another opportunity. If we use this opportunity to expand our understanding, it will not be seen as a defeat, only another chance to learn and grow!

56

No one's education is ever complete.

Only one thing is more powerful
than learning from experience, and
that is not learning from experience!

The fact that changes come into our lives means that we can be prepared to handle them courageously and triumphantly. Through life experiences, often brought about by change, we may gain mastery of our emotions, our minds and bodies, our thoughts and feelings.

The way to make conscious change, achieve new goals, and perfect our skills is through diligent practice and study on a consistent basis. This means making the commitment to develop our self-discipline and to persist and endure until the goal is met. Don't give up easily! You have the ability to make striking progress in the pursuit of your goals.

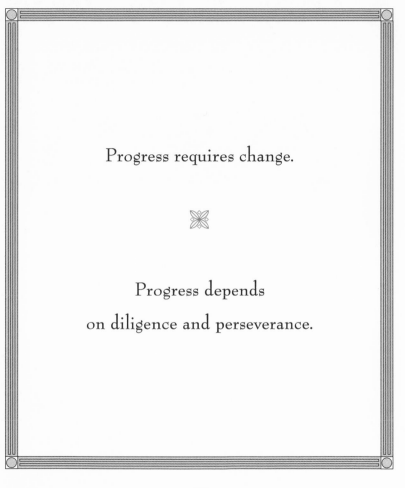

Progress requires change.

Progress depends
on diligence and perseverance.

To be an innovator, an entrepreneur, you must first recognize that you have within you the power to be creative. Next, be willing to try new experiences, to discover new fields that may offer opportunities for development. Being open and receptive can teach us much about the world and help sincere and creative individuals become innovative entrepreneurs.

Rather than being consumed with problems and limitations, we can rise above them to allow divine inspiration to guide us to better solutions. When we rule our minds in a positive way, we choose the path we want to walk down.

World progress needs entrepreneurs.

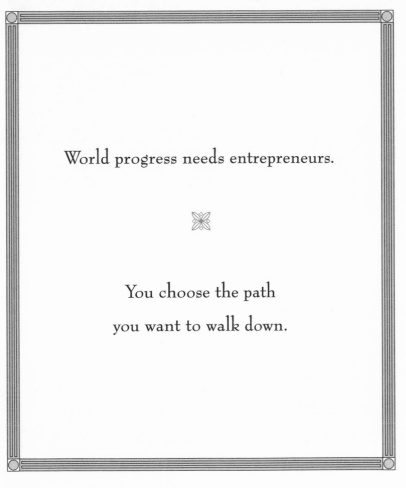

You choose the path
you want to walk down.

Dreams, visions, ideas can play significant roles in our lives. They can entice, entertain, or inspire us to greatness. To bring them into reality, however, we must act! Cowardice and lack of faith can keep one from a chosen goal, but if the heart is strong and brave, you can add action to your dreams and make them real.

Keeping an eye on the vision becomes necessary throughout the process. Focus on where you want to go, instead of where you have been. Much valuable time can be wasted in getting bogged down in past experiences or mistakes. After learning from past experiences, continue forward optimistically toward your goals.

Your dreams can come true

when you activate them.

Focus on where you want to go,

instead of where you have been.

Success

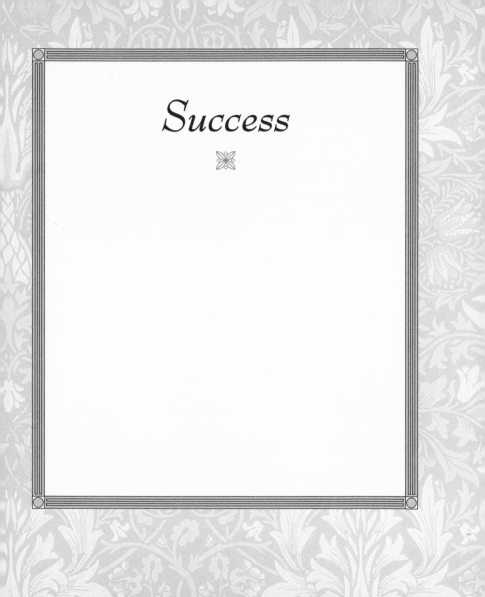

Sometimes, when we experience misfortune, if we remember that God is there in the midst of the confusion we can be better able to deal with situations in a positive, loving way. Experiences come to us for a purpose and, when we follow the guidance of the spirit within, we may find that the purpose is a good one.

We cannot have productive lives if we live with the constant fear of avoiding mistakes and misfortunes. Staying within known boundaries may avoid mistakes, but it can also prevent life from becoming rich and exciting. If you are committed to growth, you learn that each new situation finds you better able to cope with new challenges.

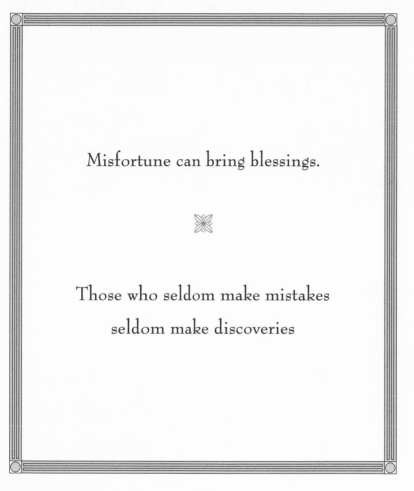

Misfortune can bring blessings.

Those who seldom make mistakes
seldom make discoveries

I*t takes courage to face the challenges of life.*

When we keep in reserve an alternate plan

for our livelihood, we can have the strength to do

whatever we need to do. Find your source.

Live from it. And keep your heart open.

Look for the positive in what may seem to be

a negative situation. Learn how to live in harmony

with others in ways that may lead to productive change.

These things are part of "being prepared"

and often lead to success.

68

Everyone should keep in reserve an
alternate plan for livelihood.

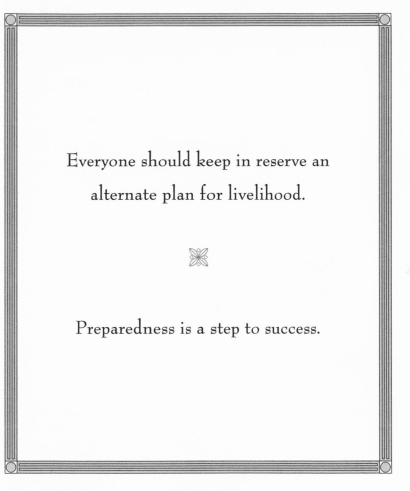

Preparedness is a step to success.

Worry is one way to meet life, but self-responsibility can be the better way. While worry stems from fear, self-responsibility comes from faith in God, faith in the goodness of life, faith in the universe, and faith in our own potential. Among the numerous ways to meet life's challenges, one of the most destructive is worrying about it.

Another way of dealing with problems is often to lash out at other people when we are feeling down. Besides causing unnecessary pain and suffering to those around us, our negative words frequently compound our own problems. How much wiser it is to hold our tongues until we can see the larger picture and know that the bad moments do pass.

Worry achieves nothing and wastes valuable time.

Destructive language tends to produce destructive results.

If we can learn to take responsibility for every area of our lives, we can also choose to create in our lives the direction and focus we need. One of the best ways to exhibit self-control is to know that faith, not fear; love, not hate; joy, not sorrow; peace, not tension; freedom, not bondage are the fundamentals of success.

Success takes practice, and if you want to feel like a success, it is important for you to begin to acknowledge your successes right now. Listen to the encouragement you receive from parents, teachers, employers, and friends. As you build on success, you may discover that you can create this again and again in various aspects of living.

Self-control leads to success.

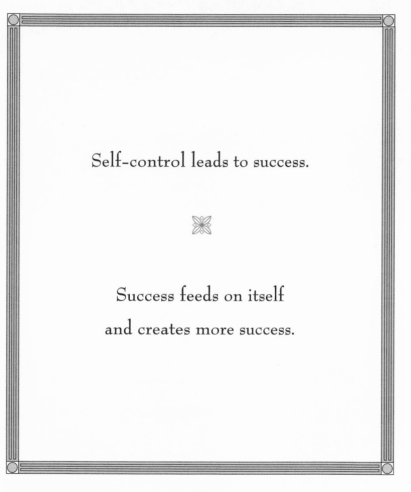

Success feeds on itself

and creates more success.

Useful
Living

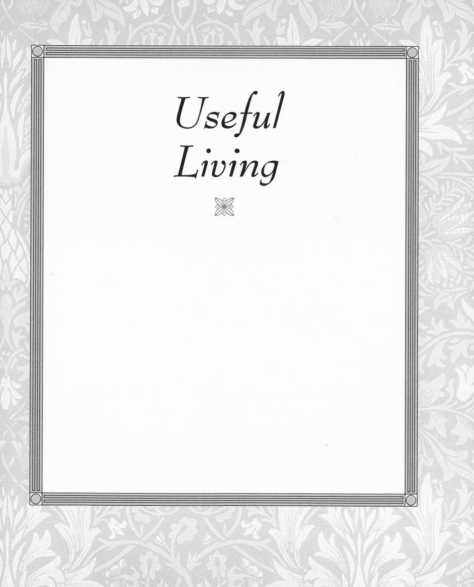

If we believe in a progressive, forward-moving existence

with wonderful potential, we will be living an interesting

life. A big difference between happiness and misery,

success and failure, effectiveness and uselessness,

cannot be blamed on circumstances or other people.

The condition of your mind creates your reality.

When the pattern of your life is woven around a positive,

generous approach to life, people will often react the same

way toward you. Our importance to others depends

on showing through our actions that we sincerely

care about them.

Nothing is interesting
if you are not interested.

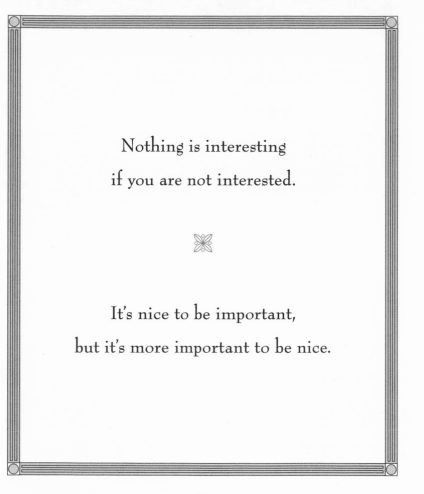

It's nice to be important,
but it's more important to be nice.

In order to be happy, healthy and stress free, it is important to believe in yourself and your individual right to happiness and health. Take time to be out of doors. The beauty of the earth can stimulate joy, thanksgiving, and healthy thoughts. Learn to laugh and to be silent. Love your children and play with your pets. Life is to be lived and enjoyed!

Probably the greatest secret to peace of mind is living the life of personal integrity—not what people think of you, but what you know of yourself. If you remain true to your ethical principles, your personal integrity can become an attractive beacon for success on every level. Listen carefully to the inner promptings of conscience and live peacefully.

Healthy minds tend to cause
healthy bodies and vice versa.

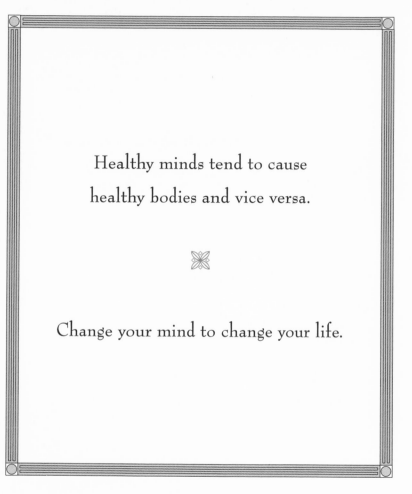

Change your mind to change your life.

Over and over we hear that giving makes it more possible to receive; however, the purpose for which we give is vital. To give with the secret hope of reward is in direct opposition to the law of love. True giving, with no strings attached, manifests love and, in the process, increases understanding. Those who do good do well.

A real economic healing activity is to tithe, or give. It is found that tithing establishes a consistent method of giving and stewarding the bounty in one's life. Through this we increase our awareness about supply, abundance, and further giving. One can observe that the family that tithes for more than ten years becomes both prosperous and happy!

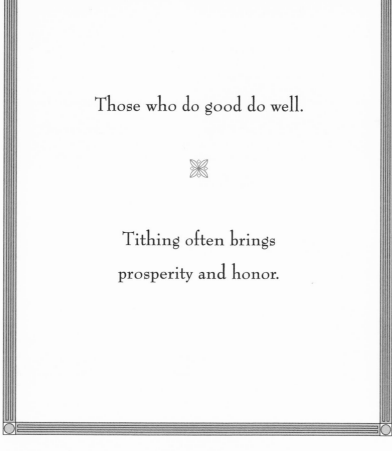

Those who do good do well.

Tithing often brings

prosperity and honor.

Much has been written about the power of the spoken word; in fact, our words are instruments of sound with which we build our world. The more we keep our word, the stronger and more creative it will be. If we say what we mean and mean what we say, our words can become the building blocks of a positive life.

As we choose to live our lives in a useful manner and in harmony with the laws of life, that which we do can be a meaningful ministry of service to others. By loving your job, holding the attitude that it may be accomplished from the perspective of doing good work for others, you are fulfilling a ministry of service. To the one who faces the light, the path is bright!

You are only as good

as your word.

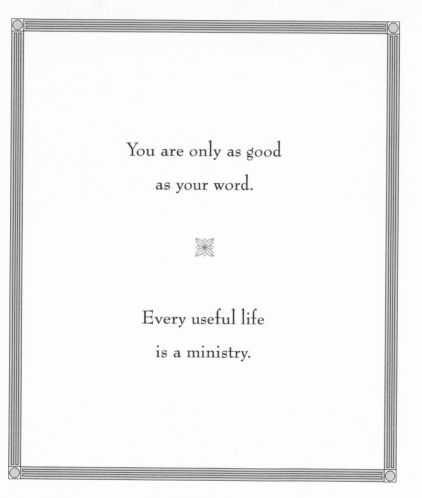

Every useful life

is a ministry.

About the Author

John Marks Templeton has led a life that speaks for itself. Born in 1912 in rural Winchester, Tennessee, he went to Yale on a scholarship and then to Oxford University as a Rhodes scholar.

He became an innovative investment counselor and went on to form very successful mutual funds—the Templeton Growth Fund and the Templeton World Fund. He was a pioneer in global investing and has been recognized for both his investing acumen as well as his personal integrity.

After retiring from the financial world in 1992, he has devoted his time to philanthropy through the Templeton Foundations. For the past twenty-five years, he has funded the Templeton Prize for Progress in Religion, the largest philanthropic prize in the world, which has been given to people such as Mother Teresa, Billy Graham, Charles Colson, and others.

He supports research that focuses on the connection between science and religion, spirituality and healing, character development, and free enterprise. He has written and edited numerous books on science and religion.